SandCastle 2

Homophones

My Deer is a Dear

Mary Elizabeth Salzmann

ABDO
Publishing Company

Published by SandCastle™, an imprint of ABDO Publishing Company, 4940 Viking Drive, Edina, Minnesota 55435.

Cover and interior photo credits: Artville, Brand X Pictures, Comstock, Corbis Images, Digital Stock, Digital Vision, Eyewire Images, PhotoDisc

Library of Congress Cataloging-in-Publication Data

Salzmann, Mary Elizabeth, 1968-
    My deer is a dear / Mary Elizabeth Salzmann.
      p. cm. -- (Homophones)
    Includes index.
    Summary: Photographs and simple text introduce homophones, words that sound alike but are spelled differently and have different meanings.
    ISBN 1-57765-652-0
    1. English language--Homonyms--Juvenile literature. [1. English language--Homonyms.]
I. Title. II. Series.

PE1595 .S26 2002
428.1--dc21

The SandCastle concept, content, and reading method have been reviewed and approved by a national advisory board including literacy specialists, librarians, elementary school teachers, early childhood education professionals, and parents.

Let Us Know

After reading the book, SandCastle would like you to tell us your stories about reading. What is your favorite page? Was there something hard that you needed help with? Share the ups and downs of learning to read. We want to hear from you! To get posted on the ABDO Publishing Company Web site, send us email at:

sandcastle@abdopub.com

About SandCastle™
Nonfiction books for the beginning reader

- Basic concepts of phonics are incorporated with integrated language methods of reading instruction. Most words are short, and phrases, letter sounds, and word sounds are repeated.

- Book levels are based on the ATOS™ for Books formula. Other considerations for readability include the number of words in each sentence, the number of characters in each word, and word lists based on curriculum frameworks.

- Full-color photography reinforces word meanings and concepts.

- "Words I Can Read" list at the end of each book teaches basic elements of grammar, helps the reader recognize the words in the text, and builds vocabulary.

- Reading levels are indicated by the number of flags on the castle.

SandCastle uses the following definitions for this series:

- Homographs: words that are spelled the same but sound different and have different meanings. *Easy memory tip: "-graph"= same look*

- Homonyms: words that are spelled and sound the same but have different meanings. *Easy memory tip: "-nym"= same name*

- Homophones: words that sound alike but are spelled differently and have different meanings. *Easy memory tip: "-phone"= sound alike*

Look for more SandCastle books in these three reading levels:

Level 1 (one flag)	**Level 2** (two flags)	**Level 3** (three flags)

Grades Pre-K to K 5 or fewer words per page	**Grades K to 1** 5 to 10 words per page	**Grades 1 to 2** 10 to 15 words per page

*Note: Some pages in this book contain more than 10 words
in order to more clearly convey the concept of the book.*

die

dye

Homophones are words that sound alike but are spelled differently and have different meanings.

This is a dense forest.

This old truck has many dents.

Duke has a dual role as pet and guard dog.

We are pretending to duel.

Nina helps make cookie
dough.

A doe is a female deer.

These two does are drinking.

Jill woke her dad up from a doze.

Our fishing trip will last for five days.

Edith is confused.

She is in a daze.

School is done.

Andrea is going home.

Dun **horses are yellow with a black mane and tail.**

He cleans an air duct in
our house.

The cat ducked into the bag.

There is dew on this leaf.

Why do I do the dishes?

(I like to help.)

Words I Can Read

Nouns

A **noun** is a person, place, or thing

air (AIR) p. 18
bag (BAG) p. 19
cat (KAT) p. 19
cookie (KUK-ee) p. 10
dad (DAD) p. 13
daze (DAYZ) p. 15
deer (DIHR) p. 11
dew (DOO) p. 20
die (DYE) p. 4

doe (DOH) p. 11
dog (DOG) p. 8
dough (DOH) p. 10
doze (DOHZ) p. 13
duct (DUHKT) p. 18
dye (DYE) p. 4
fishing (FISH-ing) p. 14
forest (FOR-ist) p. 6
guard (GARD) p. 8

house (HOUSS) p. 18
leaf (LEEF) p. 20
mane (MAYN) p. 17
pet (PET) p. 8
role (ROHL) p. 8
school (SKOOL) p. 16
tail (TAYL) p. 17
trip (TRIP) p. 14
truck (TRUHK) p. 7

Plural Nouns

A **plural noun** is more than one
person, place, or thing

days (DAYZ) p. 14
dents (DENTSS) p. 7
dishes (DISH-ez) p. 21
does (DOHZ) p. 12

homophones
(HOME-uh-fonez)
p. 5
horses (HORSS-ez)
p. 17

meanings
(MEE-ningz) p. 5
words (WURDZ) p. 5

Proper Nouns

A proper noun is the name of a person, place, or thing

Andrea (AN-dree-uh) p. 16

Duke (DOOK) p. 8
Edith (EE-dith) p. 15

Jill (JIL) p. 13
Nina (NEE-nuh) p. 10

Verbs

A verb is an action or being word

are (AR) pp. 5, 9, 12, 17
cleans (KLEENZ) p. 18
do (DOO) p. 21
drinking (DRINGK-ing) p. 12
ducked (DUHKT) p. 19
duel (DOO-uhl) p. 9

going (GOH-ing) p. 16
has (HAZ) pp. 7, 8
have (HAV) p. 5
help (HELP) p. 21
helps (HELPSS) p. 10
is (IZ) pp. 6, 11, 15, 16, 20
last (LAST) p. 14

like (LIKE) p. 21
make (MAKE) p. 10
pretending (pri-TEND-ing) p. 9
sound (SOUND) p. 5
spelled (SPELD) p. 5
will (WIL) p. 14
woke (WOHK) p. 13

Adjectives

An adjective describes something

alike (uh-LIKE) p. 5
black (BLAK) p. 17
confused (kuhn-FYOOZD) p. 15
dense (DENSS) p. 6
different (DIF-ur-uhnt) p. 5

done (DUHN) p. 16
dual (DOO-uhl) p. 8
dun (DUHN) p. 17
female (FEE-male) p. 11
five (FIVE) p. 14
her (HUR) p. 13

many (MEN-ee) p. 7
old (OHLD) p. 7
our (OUR) pp. 14, 18
these (THEEZ) p. 12
this (THISS) pp. 7, 20
two (TOO) p. 12
yellow (YEL-oh) p. 17

23

Match these homophones to the pictures

 dear
deer

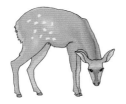 doe
dough

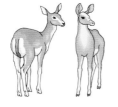 does
doze

 ducked
duct